River Willows: Senryu from Lockdown

River Willows:
Senryu from Lockdown

by
Tony Ullyatt

River Willows: Senryū from Lockdown

Dryad Press (Pty) Ltd
Postnet Suite 281, Private Bag X16,
Constantia, 7848, Cape Town, South Africa
www.dryadpress.co.za
business@dryadpress.co.za

Copyright © poems Tony Ullyatt
All rights reserved

No part of this book may be reproduced or transmitted in
any form or by any electronic or mechanical means, including
photocopying and recording, or any other information storage
or retrieval system, without written permission from the
publisher or copyright holder

Cover design and typography: Stephen Symons
Editor: Michèle Betty
Copy Editor: Helena Janisch

Set in 9.5/14pt Palatino Linotype

First published in Cape Town by Dryad Press (Pty) Ltd, 2020

ISBN 978-1-990983-26-9

Visit www.dryadpress.co.za to read more about all our books
and to buy them. You will also find features, links to author
interviews and news of author events. Follow our social
media platforms on Instagram and Facebook to be the first to
hear about our new releases.

in memory of my Gisela
who came to mean so much to so many

INTRODUCTION

It began as a small project to keep myself occupied during lockdown: to try to write a senryū each day about some happening of that day. After eighty-three days, I stopped with 111 senryū complete.

Although the plan was for just one senryū a day, sometimes two or three would happen. These were often separate pieces with no links between them; they appear here in the traditional three-line, 5-7-5-syllable senryū or haiku form.

On other occasions, however, two or three senryū were linked by virtue of their subject. In such instances, these senryū are not cast in their traditional format, but take on the structure of a quasi-epode: a first long line followed by a second, shorter line. However, each 'stanza' still contains seventeen syllables: twelve in the first line and five in the second.

Each of these small poems was intended as a record of its particular day. Some came to mind early in the day, at or before sunrise, while others waited until late at night.

I have refrained from indulging in excessive editing and/or revision, primarily because that would defeat the underlying intention of writing the day's senryū *about* that day *in* that day. Consequently, the tone, structure and language vary considerably throughout the collection – but then, so did the days during lockdown.

The collection opens with a Praeludium: nine senryū written shortly before lockdown in late February 2020, when Gisela and I were in Stellenbosch to launch her first book of poems.

Tony Ullyatt
17 June 2020

*poetry has
one subject, impermanence*
A R Ammons

PRAELUDIUM

THE STELLENBOSCH SENRYŪ

for Gisela on setting her doves free

28 February 2020

>even before dawn
>morning's birdsong has begun:
>I've time to listen

>sunrise gilds oak leaves
>wind swirling tumult through them:
>poems everywhere

29 February 2020

>a speckled pigeon
>lands on the balcony chair:
>the day's good omen

>from dawn a pigeon
>chanting its five-note mantra:
>leap year's harbinger

1 March 2020

> desiccated brown
> oak leaves and drought-withered green
> dance to the wind's whim

2 March 2020

> in Andringa Street
> just past Church Street, an oak tree
> with pigeons shitting
>
> in pre-dawn's glimmer
> silhouettes long for daylight
> to flaunt their textures
>
> the oak's silhouette
> waits for the sunrise to light
> its third dimension
>
> two floors up I sit
> in the wingback chair: day breaks
> tinged with fresh coffee

LOCKDOWN

The Day Before

>coronavirus
>fills the world's news; kills folks too:
>when will it get here?

Day 1

>when this lockdown's done
>I might make hibernation
>my fulltime career

Day 2

>in this trying time
>with street and mailbox empty
>the cape robin calls

Day 3

>brindled grey-white clouds
>display no urge to move on:
>the sun can't shine through

Day 4

>through these vexing days
>the letterbox lies quite bare:
>such pleasure in that!

Day 5

> behind the day's heat
> clouds unleash a thunderstorm:
> later the slug called

Day 6

> to the rain's rhythms
> pink bells of hibiscus sway
> bright beside wet leaves

Day 7

> confined by four walls
> inconvenience galore:
> no greater freedom

> shopping yesterday
> some shelves stripped or almost so:
> hysterics well stocked

> wild things don't complain
> but humans do once they queue:
> who built the cities?

Day 8

> in the pitch-black dark
> nature's call held a surprise:
> the loo lid was down!

> with our curtains wide
> the sun like a drunk driver
> crashed in wrecklessly

Day 9

> a hot summer's day
> in the middle of autumn:
> we'll curse winter too

Day 10

> in lockdown's stillness
> a quite unfamiliar sound:
> a car driving past

Day 11

> Holy Week begins
> with the virus still present:
> how blessed our lives are

Day 12

fewer cars but more
drivers ignoring the rules
who entitled them?

Day 13

in morning's pale sun:
the grass grows, the orchid blooms
I drink tea, dunk rusks

on my plate an ant
discovers last night's dried crumbs
then samples my tea

Day 14

inside and outside
have acquired new meanings:
illness builds blockades

panic buyers surge
before Easter and Christmas:
faith and greed embrace

Day 15

    morning I drink tea
    an ant grooms itself neatly:
    joy in the moment

Day 16

    breathe in [   ] breathe out [   ] check
    birds, sun, trees, clouds, thunder, pain:
    so you're still alive

    with the sun rising
    stars dwindle in its brightness:
    they'll be there at dusk

Day 17

    I gaze at the stars:
    there is nothing between us
    but millions of years

Day 18

    identical days
    trail one after the other:
    each unlike the rest

Day 19

>trees can't clutch the wind
>or recall every bird's song:
>transience persists

>as the world dons masks
>thieves are not perplexed; they wear
>dark balaclavas

Day 20

>the morning brightens
>after the night's steady rain:
>mist drapes the river

Day 21

>when life leaves no choice
>it makes things much easier:
>that's the route to take

Day 22

    in cahoots with night
    winter pilfers daylight's hours:
    birds start later too

    in the pre-dawn oak
    the cape robin celebrates
    the joy of freedom

    dawn's colours exceed
    the scope of words; awareness
    depends on silence

    the only rewards
    for stupidity are death
    or grief: you must choose . . .

Day 23

    through the night some rain
    toward twelve the slug popped in
    flaunting its freedom

Day 24

after Bashō

what song might the leaves
and blossoms sing as they fall,
their purpose fulfilled?

my wife sleeps; her hand
on my shoulder as we share
lockdown's gentle touch

Day 25

towns and cities now
flaunt their Edward Hopper streets:
coffee shops shut too

my neighbour's mower
seems intrusively noisy
in these quiet days

the supermarket
car park's packed, lockdown ignored:
the death wish triumphs

Day 26

    around four-thirty
    I wake sweating profusely:
    low blood sugar strikes

    with these sundrenched days
    summer's message is quite clear:
    it's not over yet

    a platoon of ants
    single-file toward the door:
    winter's some way off

Day 27

    nine days to the end
    assuming no extensions:
    storms don't have schedules

Day 28

    these days when nothing
    of importance comes about:
    what splendid stillness!

Day 29

    is today the day
    no senryū gets written?
    wind rustling through leaves

Day 30

    for Michèle

    the orchid's last bloom
    fluttered down some days ago:
    a new leaf sprouting

    a fine drizzle comes
    thunderheads mass beyond hills:
    monochrome splendour

Day 31

    after brusque jostling
    in shops with payday people:
    the refuge of home

Day 32

> *Listening to Mahler's Ninth Symphony: IV Adagio*

storms wrench out stout trees
rose petals drifting earthward:
ways to say farewell

Day 33

rain taps privet leaves:
how good it would be to hear
their elusive song

white-eyes chirp flirting
despite the wind's dull bluster:
life with no lockdown

Day 34

I long to escape from myself with good reason:
but where can I go?

trees rustle, birds call, I hear no other voices:
is that an answer?

Day 35

> the end is no end:
> some tighter restraints loosened
> as if nature cared

Day 36

> May arrived today
> walking jogging biking in:
> life remains fragile

> back garden morning
> dandelion clock, drowned mole:
> autumn and winter

Day 37

> throughout lockdown days
> police, ambulance sirens:
> life's consistencies

Day 38

> Sunday's shelves plundered
> others' haste leaves me breathless:
> a day of what rest?

Day 39

>   you pack your suitcase
>   for the unwelcome journey
>   on pain's chance roster

Day 40

>   the hospital's like
>   an airport departures lounge:
>   you travel alone

Day 41

>   each room of the house
>   feels huge despite its clutter:
>   they miss your presence

>   wanting to show you
>   something I head for the lounge:
>   you're in hospital

Day 42

>   a golden morning
>   then a cloud-grey afternoon:
>   weather's shifting moods

Day 43

> much like a virus
> rowdiness breaks out again:
> tranquil days succumb

Day 44

> a murder weapon
> is what a car becomes when
> the driver's loaded

Day 45

> watched grass grow, drank tea
> heard a soft breeze ruffling leaves:
> a busy morning

Day 46

> sunrise prompts sunshine
> until sunset and bright stars:
> a marvellous day

Day 47

> overblown roses
> petals float gently to earth:
> an ordinary day

Day 48

>the cacophony
>of undiscipline resumes:
>death has been waiting

Day 49

>mountain streams follow
>the path of least resistance:
>but they aren't human

Day 50

>fine poetry breeds
>in mediocrity's muck:
>lotuses in mud

>gusty winds braiding
>next door's clothes with the wash line:
>nature's quaint lockdown

Day 51

>days and dates are lost
>in repetitious routines:
>rivers don't count drops

Day 52

> what is the difference
> between a gift and a bribe?
> nothing but timing

Day 53

> the river's glass-flat
> waters pristine as stillness:
> the idyll short-lived

Day 54

> a cloud-brindled sky
> somewhere the smell of incense:
> the day's sheer pleasures

Day 55

> a gaggle of birds
> quite lovely to listen to
> and envy as well

Day 56

> lockdown paradox:
> parking's never hard to find
> though queues seem longer

Day 57

> neglect and dust are
> filling the office slowly
> as acquaintance leaves

Day 58

> eighty senryū
> fifty-eight days of constraint:
> quality wavers

Day 59

> for fifty-nine days
> itching like a mangy dog:
> beard yields to smooth blade

Day 60

> grey clouds edged with gold
> trees writhe as though they're possessed:
> winter's harbingers

Day 61

> today's mail box holds
> an account and a letter:
> a routine restored

Day 62

>   doctors' rooms are where
>   you are compelled to listen
>   to music you loathe

Day 63

>   a long colonnade
>   peopled by bad memories:
>   an unwelcome dream

Day 64

>   the slug came last night
>   stayed to eat his fill then left:
>   no permit needed

Day 65

>   pain's a lonely thing
>   in the relentless pursuit
>   of its stubborn needs

Day 66

> at the traffic light
> they stand with a board PLEASE HELP
> then she faints, he screams
>
> his face fraught with fear
> he drags her to the pavement:
> praying she won't die
>
> not here, please not here
> not outside Johnny's Café
> the gawping riff-raff

Day 67

> bottlestores teeming
> a wonderful day to be
> a teetotaller

Day 68

> inevitable
> the devastations of drink:
> birds chanting vespers

Day 69

>harsh light of sunrise
>bleaching dawn's azures and pinks
>to limpid paleness

Day 70

>in the evening mist
>haloes circle the street lamps:
>sanctity far off

Day 71

>dawn is quick to warm:
>tardy shoppers stand and sweat
>in long sluggish queues

Day 72

>coronavirus
>a democratic disease
>no one is exempt

Day 73

>we watched an eagle
>high up in the silky oak
>until he flew off

Day 74

>some days bring it on
>creative constipation:
>and it shows later

>a mask on the chin:
>it's hard to explain to some
>where nose and mouth are

Day 75

>a mole's been making
>a hill on our lawn; no one's
>made a mountain yet

>officious people
>doing the work they're meant to
>aren't doing favours

>seventy-five days
>one hundred senryū done
>some mediocre

Day 76

>the dried pine needles
>of the forest floor crunching
>whole worlds underfoot

Day 77

> I bought panini
> to remember those hard times
> and the splendid views

Day 78

> the place we start from
> and the place we arrive at
> may not be our choice

Day 79

> the early sun peers
> like an inquisitive child
> with a winter stare
>
> pain finds its own way
> along quaint trails and old paths
> back to your front door

Day 80

> dying's not something
> we should get accustomed to
> but for kind release

Day 81

Gisela's birthday

let's forget the way
things might well or should have been:
each day's what matters

Day 82

it happens these days:
my mind slips its tight harness:
turbulent silence

Day 83

after the storm's passed
the soil and rain's smell lingers:
nothing's permanent